Rebuilding Trust:

Activities and Techniques for Guided Therapy to Bring Back Intimacy, Love, and Trust in Your Relationship

By

Andrew E. Ferrell

Disclaimer

Rebuilding trust provide the tools to tackle every sort of stressful situation and anticipate and end meltdowns before they even begin.

Inside this book, you'll learn simple strategies and tips on how to control your emotions for life, then sit, relax, and stay tuned for these life-changing strategies.

TABLE OF CONTENT:

Rebuilding Trust:

INTRODUCTION:

the start of the relationship's collapse

Rebuilding trust

It concerns the relationship between the parents.

Everything began with such noble goals. If kids were going to come, they were going to get the finest possible treatment. love, care, focus, and assistance.

What a lovely and excellent beginning. Family life then started. It was necessary to grow the nuclear family and take on job away from home. Place bread on the table, ideally with a few more here and there. For instance, a vacation and pleasant things. And the "regularities" of daily life: picking clothes, listening to concerns, assisting with homework, mediating conflicts, consoling, etc.

It turns out to be quite the task, gradually. Since they require a great deal of time and attention, to be honest. However, that is part of the deal, is it not? Indeed, In the partnership, there are indications of mutual annoyance, but they are quickly dismissed. "It's okay, it's only a part of the arrangement." There is enough diversion from the job, the sport, the club, or whatever else. Seldom is there time for meaningful discussions and a nice get-together. "Jacob, that is how things are right now!" Everyone is aware, of course, that sex is getting harder to have. "We stop doing it if the kids are at home."

I ask every couple seated across from me, "When was the last time you did something together, properly together?" because there's a chance that things will get stagnant. I could create a book on the solutions. 99 percent don't hold up. Both spouses realize this in their hearts. All of the answers are regarding "special needs children," "difficult behavior," "they really can't be alone," "no support outside the family," and "as long as they are having a good time, then so am I," and so forth.

Though managing the family is necessary, parents' primary responsibility should be to inspire and guide their family instead of managing it. And the most crucial element of a happy, healthy family life—where kids grow up "like crazy"—is a household where the parents

Rebuilding trust

prioritize one another above all else.

similar to the welcome home greeting. As a parent, you should always welcome your partner first, regardless of how much your kids try to dance around you and get your attention. Children who see this action daily learn about confidence-boosting affection. the love that gave rise to them. Parents who witness these kids leaving the house in the future will have an amazing experience.

CHARTER 1:

Reestablish safety in building a safe relationship space:

In a close relationship, trust is based on feeling secure in the other person. Be it lies, infidelity, or broken promises, these things can seriously erode trust between spouses. Still, that doesn't always indicate a relationship isn't worth saving. Rebuilding trust after a serious breach can be difficult, but it is achievable with both partners' commitment to the process.

Gathering the Pieces

Regaining the sense of security required for a relationship to flourish and evolve requires a lot of time and work. For many couples trying to get back on track, the sticking point is often in recovering from the trauma of a breach in trust requirement for a connection to prosper and keep expanding. For many couples trying to get back on track, the sticking point is often in recovering from the trauma of a breach of trust.

According to research, for a couple to successfully move past a trust violation, they need to address the following five sources of contention.

- Being aware of specifics

- Letting go of the rage

- Exhibiting dedication

- Establishing trust again

- Mend the connection

To mend, whether you were the betrayer or the spouse who committed the offense the trust

Rebuilding trust

in your partnership, you both need to recommit to each other and your relationship.

Understand the Specifics

There are always two sides to any story, even ones that appear to be quite obvious. The partner who is at fault should provide their partner with clear answers to all concerns and be forthright and honest with information.

The deceived party will gain a more comprehensive picture of the circumstances as a result. What, where, and when did it happen? What emotions or issues might have played a role in this circumstance? Which circumstances mitigated the situation?

Let Go of Your Anger

Even small betrayals of trust can cause issues with one's physical, mental, and emotional well-being. Partners may experience sleep difficulties or lose appetite. They could become easily angered or agitated over little matters.

Betrayed partners must pay attention to and consider all of their feelings, even if it may be tempting to repress all of their anger and emotions. Think about how the betrayal of your relationship will affect you and other people.

Consider how life has been thrown off, as well as all the concerns and uncertainties that are starting to surface. Tell your lover about all of these emotions.

It's even suggested that the offending partner express whatever anger and resentment they've been holding inside since the occurrence.

Be Dedicated

It's possible that both parties—especially the one who feels deceived—are doubting their dedication to the union and wondering if it can ever be saved.

Empathic actions can be restorative for both parties since they allow for the recognition

Rebuilding trust

and validation of injured sentiments as well as the sharing of sorrow, frustration, and rage as well as regret and remorse.

Building on this, outlining what each party expects from the relationship can assist in helping partners realize that moving forward in a relationship entails clear expectations that each party has committed to meeting.

To maintain a commitment to keeping the relationship going, both partners must collaborate in defining what is necessary.

When conveying this, stay away from employing When expressing what you see, expect, or desire from your spouse, avoid using terms that could lead to conflict, such as always, must, never, or should. Rather, utilize non-blaming "I" expressions and language that encourage candid discussion. Take "I need to feel like a priority in your life" as an example rather than "You never put me first."

Reestablishing Confidence

Setting clear objectives and reasonable deadlines together will help you get your relationship back on track. Understand that restoring trust is a process that involves patience and the following:

Choose to extend forgiveness or accept forgiveness. Decide to love by making an effort to let go of the past. Adhering to this aim is crucial, even though reaching its entirety can need some time.

• Remain receptive to personal development. You are unable to fix shattered trust with mere words of forgiveness and assurances. For the issues to remain dormant, both spouses must determine, investigate, and address the root causes of the betrayal.

• Communicate your ideas and be conscious of your deepest emotions. It won't fix anything to let one side focus endlessly on the circumstance or deed that betrayed the trust. Rather, it's critical to communicate honestly about the specifics and let out all of your grief and rage.

Rebuilding trust

• Desire for it to succeed. More lies or lip service have no place in this process. Be truthful and sincere in your intentions.

After everyone has absorbed the aforementioned advice, be transparent about your objectives, and follow up frequently should confirm that you are on course.

How to Help Couples Restore Trust in Their Partnership

should provide clear answers to all of their partner's inquiries and be forthright and honest while providing facts.

The deceived party will gain a more comprehensive picture of the circumstances as a result. What, where, and when did it happen? What emotions or issues might have played a role in this circumstance? Which circumstances mitigated the situation?

Regarding the Offender

Reminding yourself of your transgressions as the one who jeopardized the relationship could be difficult or even unpleasant. But keep in mind that the aforementioned actions are necessary for the healing and restoration process. While you're working with them:

If you were the one who lied, cheated, or betrayed trust in your relationship, demonstrate that the bad conduct has stopped by acting differently. That implies that there will be no more lies, secrets, adultery, or similar things. From now on, always be straightforward, honest, and upfront.

• Be truthful and make an effort to determine the cause of the inappropriate behavior. Phrases like "I don't know" don't give you confidence or assist you in identifying the problem's core cause.

• Accept accountability for your deeds and choices; express regret for any harm you may have caused; and refrain from becoming defensive, as this will only exacerbate the situation. It is likewise ineffective to defend

Rebuilding trust

your actions by pointing to what your partner is doing or has done in the past.

For Those Who Have Betrayed

While your ability to go forward is mostly dependent on what your partner can demonstrate to you, keep in mind that your ability to succeed as greatly depends on the effort you make. As you move on, each day:

• Attempt to ascertain what went wrong in the relationship before the actual betrayal and why. You won't be able to forget what happened, but you might be able to acquire the answers you need to move on.

• After you've committed to giving your spouse another chance, give them consistent feedback on things that make them happy or feel good by responding positively and offering encouragement.

• Recognize that it's acceptable to decide to end the relationship after giving it some thought to the preceding actions or starting them. Just be sincere with both your partner and yourself, and don't act a certain way just because you think it's what a committed partner expects from you.

Regarding the Pair

As you work alone, don't forget to give each other your full attention. Remind each other that you all deserve truthful, forthright responses to the inquiries you have concerning the betrayal.

Reestablishing Communication

Couples need to focus on approaching their relationship as though it were brand-new after they have committed to restoring trust. Instead of assuming their spouse knows what they want out of the blue, both parties need to ask for what they need.

Don't lose faith in this new partnership, even though it is in the company of the same individual.

Rebuilding trust

Refusing to trust someone out of fear or rage will keep you from emotionally reestablishing a connection with them. This prevents the healthy progression of your connection.

Rather, make the necessary efforts to reestablish mutual support and trust to work toward mending the relationship. Decide together what, to you both, constitutes a healthy relationship.

Establishing date nights, working on a five-, ten-, or even twenty-year plan together, figuring out your love languages, and periodically checking in with your partner to see how things are going are a few examples.

Recall that maintaining a relationship takes work. Even the closest of couples must put forth a lot of effort at rekindling the flame and striving to advance in tandem, year after year.

Seeking Expert Assistance

If you address the five concerns mentioned above and remember that getting through this is only possible if you stay strong and resolve to work on it together, you may work on creating a healthier, happier, and more honest relationship.

To help the two of you move on, a therapist can assist you in understanding the what, why, and how of what transpired.

To better understand the reasons behind the breach of trust, both parties must be willing to pursue counseling. However, you could also need or want to look into individual treatment in addition to couples counseling.

There are numerous methods of care available for Particularly beneficial couples that aim to restore connection, trust, and communication. After going through such a crisis, you can even find that your relationship is stronger as a result of ongoing effort and treatment.

Last observation

In a secure relationship, you experience love, trust, and value.

Rebuilding trust

It is your right to be truly happy in any relationship, therefore making sure you and your partner feel safe should come first.

In a relationship, safety encompasses both emotional and physical security. You can fully trust your mates and have a deeper understanding of them when you feel comfortable around them. As it should be, you also feel safe and vulnerable around them.

It is crucial to communicate openly with your partner; you can Do that only in a relationship where there is emotional safety.

Five indicators that something is amiss in a partnership

The following are some overt indicators that you don't feel secure in your relationship:

1. You're hesitant to show affection

When you're the only one in the relationship who initiates contact, you could grow weary of trying to get in touch with your spouse. If you try to initiate intimacy with your spouse and they reject you, the problem could get worse.

After you've experienced this rejection a few times, you could find it difficult to communicate with them. If nothing changes, you'll quickly notice that you're slipping apart. This demonstrates that the partnership lacks emotional stability.

2. It's easy to ignore or mock your worries.

To feel secure in a relationship, you must be able to express your sentiments to your spouse. When your partner does anything inappropriate or uncomfortable, you need to tell them about your worries and let them know how you feel.

When you disclose things with your spouse, though, you can discover that they don't even acknowledge your feelings. You can get insecure as a result and be reluctant to voice your worries in the future.

Rebuilding trust

3. You're terrified to part from your spouse.

If you have trouble letting your partner go to events or go on trips with pals, you should examine the extent of your faith in them.

While wanting to spend quality time with your partner is acceptable, maintaining a successful relationship also requires giving each other some space.

You should question yourself why you feel this way if you find that you always want to be with your spouse, know what they're doing, or know where they are when you're not around.

These could be indicators that anything they've done to you in the past is making you feel unsafe around them. It might also be the outcome of resentment or long-standing problems unrelated to your relationship.

4. Your spouse makes threats of divorcing or breaking up with you.

Mind games are useful in a variety of methods. Occasionally, when you bring up an important topic with your partner, they may threaten to leave or file for divorce.

This could be their strategy for keeping you bound to them despite your feelings of insecurity in the partnership.

You should be free to open up to your partner about your feelings in a stable relationship without worrying about manipulation or the possibility of divorce or separation.

5. You surveil your spouse.

In a relationship, what does it mean to feel safe? When you feel comfortable in a relationship, you can be sure that your spouse won't do you any harm on purpose.

If you consistently fall behind your Investigating your partner's whereabouts behind your back

Rebuilding trust

when you're not around may indicate that you don't feel secure in your partnership.

Spying on their partner's devices is something people undertake to validate long-standing concerns. Recognize the motivation behind this action first.

Recognize whether it's because your boyfriend has cheated on you in the past.

It's clear that emotional stability hasn't returned to the relationship, therefore you should feel comfortable confiding in your partner.

What qualities in a partner give someone a sense of security?

You may notice certain behaviors in your partner that reassure you that you are safe together. In most cases, these emotions and traits come easily to them. These are a portion of them.

1. Safety of the body

Your partner doesn't take advantage of your physical strength advantage. Nonetheless, their warmth and affection reassure you.

Your partner won't hit you or threaten you with physical harm in a physically secure relationship.

They are gentle and accepting when you reach out to them; they will never put any pressure on you, either emotionally or sexually. Additionally, you don't run when they reach for you since you feel secure with them.

2. Confidence

A vital component of safe and secure interactions is trust. It's When your partner consistently casts doubt on you, it is tough to truly trust them.

Try talking to them when they continue doing things that make you wonder where you fit into their lives. You can always find

Rebuilding trust

safety in a relationship based on trust, so if something starts to feel awkward, tell your spouse.

3. Sincerity

You cannot establish a safe relationship with someone you are dishonest with. Building solid, long-lasting partnerships isn't the best approach to lying about things you could easily inform your spouse.

Be honest with your partner about any situation, no matter how serious you believe it to be. When you're in a relationship with someone who never stops lying, it can be nearly impossible to feel secure to you.

4. Weakness

You don't have to worry about your spouse using your anxieties or insecurities against you if you are totally honest and transparent with them.

You gradually come to feel safe with your lover when you are open and vulnerable with them.

Even though they are aware of your difficulties and fears, you have faith that they won't take deliberate actions to harm you.

5. Reliability

You feel secure in your knowledge of your spouse since you already know what to anticipate from them and how they will respond in particular circumstances.

Nothing surprises you once more because you can practically gauge your partner's response to certain situations.

6. Respect for one another

An essential component of any happy relationship is respect. When making decisions, your spouse ought to take your sentiments into account in addition to their own. Because it serves as a constant reminder that they think highly of you, you feel safe in a relationship where they respect you.

Rebuilding trust

7. Eavesdropping

You need to be with someone who is supportive and validates you on your journey to feeling safe in a relationship, especially when what you're going through saying is comparable to nonsensical speech.

Avoid unhealthy behavior by listening to your partner and understanding their perspective before starting a pointless dispute.

Relationships that last the longest and are in the best condition are those where both partners have decided to use and practice active listening.

8. Being authentic

Even if it might not thrill everyone around you, being brutally honest defines who you are. You have to be real and not back down as you learn how to feel secure in a partnership.

You shouldn't have to hide or pretend to be someone you're not in a stable relationship.

An understanding partner can save your life because you know that you won't expect a blow-up in return when you express yourself.

You also know that your partner is being completely honest with you and isn't withholding anything significant from you.

9. Gratitude

Instead of attempting to alter you, your spouse offers guidance or inspiration to improve upon who you are. They want the best for you, therefore this doesn't necessarily mean they're attempting to dominate your life.

They consider your welfare before offering any guidance. Since you both feel comfortable being yourself and are committed to each other, you don't need to alter who you are or your entire being for your spouse to improve with each day that goes by.

10. Interaction

Rebuilding trust

An essential component of any secure connection is effective communication. To enable you to collaborate with your partner to find a solution, be honest with them about the things that make you feel uneasy or nervous.

The quickest method to resolve a relationship problem is to talk to your partner.

The value of having a secure relationship

Every individual has a basic desire for protection, regardless of whether they are in our daily lives or our relationships.

Similar to the actual world, when we don't feel safe enough, we naturally look for safety. Relationships are no different. There is always space for development and progress in a relationship when we feel protected.

You attempt to be better versions of yourself and learn more about yourself when you feel safe in a relationship.

Relationships bring with them a variety of emotions that, if you don't take the time to comprehend, could become too much to handle.

Relationship safety and receiving approval from your spouse are crucial. In a relationship, you instinctively feel confident and have faith in your spouse when there is safety.

Because you know they value your presence, you feel safe and comfortable with your spouse when you feel wanted by them They wouldn't intentionally do anything to harm you.

In a relationship, feeling safe is not having to worry about your spouse treating you disrespectfully or not considering your feelings. In this manner, you can enjoy the happiness that comes with knowing that you're in a safe place and avoid drowning in self-doubt every day.

What steps can you take to ensure your safety in the relationship?

Rebuilding trust

It's time to take care of things on your own after discussing some issues that don't seem safe in your relationship with your partner.

There are various actions you can take to better your circumstances. You can experiment with several strategies until you find one that works for you.

You can take the following actions to feel secure in your relationship:

1. Recognize it

First, acknowledge that you deserve safety in a relationship and that it does exist. Recognize that you deserve better and that it is not ideal to feel insecure in a relationship.

2. Take some time out of the house.

Try taking your significant other somewhere new. To become more at ease and secure in their presence in public, you could choose to see a movie or go on a date night.

You usually don't consider the strains in your relationship when you're out with your significant other. You both concentrate on enjoying yourselves; every relationship needs this break.

3. Establish limits in your partnership.

Being honest and vulnerable in a relationship doesn't always mean you should tolerate rudeness.

Inform your partner and set clear limits if you're uncomfortable showing love in public or if you'd rather not talk about a particular subject with them.

Make it obvious to your spouse if you don't want to discuss your previous relationships, for instance.

Maybe you should reconsider that relationship if they don't respect your requests, as it indicates that they don't know what it is to be safe in a relationship.

4. Form a support group that consists of individuals other than your spouse.

To talk to individuals you can trust about your relationship issues, you can start a support group.

You can confide in your support group to feel safe and independent when you need someone to listen to you through a difficult time in your relationship other than your partner.

You feel more secure and less anxious when you know that you can depend on yourself to handle any problems in your relationship These problems usually go away.

5. Express your emotions honestly

You should be open and honest with your spouse about your feelings if you're unhappy with some aspects of the relationship or would like to chat with them more.

Your partner won't be able to relate to you unless you are honest with them; occasionally, they won't know what's on your mind unless you express it.

After communicating your feelings to your partner, if nothing seems to change, you might want to give the relationship another look.

What does your relationship require for you to feel secure?

A few things must be in place for a person to feel comfortable in a relationship. Here are a few of them:

1. Having a support system

Some come from dysfunctional households where parents, for various reasons such as mental health issues or addictions, never seemed to follow through on their commitments.

Rebuilding trust

As a result, kids instinctively learn to rely only on those whose only goal is to serve them—that is, on themselves and their caretaker.

They may give the impression that they don't trust their spouse enough to confide in them and share their troubles since they find it difficult to rely on anyone, even their partner.

Even though you are addicted to being by yourself, you need to let go and make room for your spouse to support you. Right now, remind yourself that the world is no longer against you. Your companion is there to support you. Permit them entry.

2. Recognization

You may have heard in the past that you should ignore your emotions or accept things as they are, but you need to let go of such ideas and prioritize your needs.

In this manner, you learn to truly enjoy your relationships and feel safer making decisions.

Remember that your partner loves and accepts you. When you know you're with someone who loves and accepts you for who you are, rather than who they wish you were, you might feel comfortable in a relationship.

3. Address issues as a group

In a relationship, you and your spouse should, at the very least, somewhat share the same ambitions and goals. You can now delegate tasks to others and stop doing everything by yourself. If you let them in, your partner is always prepared to lend a hand.

Instead of attempting to win points when you confront problems in your relationship, try to work as a team to find a solution.

What does it mean to be secure in a relationship?

Rebuilding trust

Building an intimate and healthy relationship based on trust requires a sense of safety in the other person.

Because there is a strong connection between the two of you, when you feel that you and your partner are one, you automatically feel comfortable in their presence.

You feel that your partner knows you better in an emotionally stable relationship since they are aware of every aspect of your life and still accept you for who you are.

Eventually, as your confidence grows, you start to open up to your spouse and confide in them about your issues and worries.

Even if your partner isn't physically close to you, you can still feel secure in your relationship because you know they care about you and trust you.

There is trust and a strong connection between you, so your partnership can be a secure place to return to after you both go out and lead independent lives.

Last observation

Safety is one of the main objectives of relationships. A secure partnership makes you happy and reduces stress.

Don't be scared to show your vulnerability and allow your spouse to get to know you better.

If you don't tell your partner how you feel, one day it can get to be too much for you. So speak up when you're wrong. For a safe relationship, you can go cautiously or even get help.

Being emotionally available to your spouse, listening to and honoring their decisions, honoring your word, resolving disagreements courteously and civilly, and being dependable are all ways to create an emotionally safe relationship.

It also takes time to feel safe in a relationship. Together with your partner's assistance and

Rebuilding trust

participation, you must consciously work toward it.

CHARTER 2:

 Cultivate self awareness in a relationship:

What is self-awareness? And how can you cultivate it?

Although we often believe we are self-aware, we are not. Here's how to improve in that area.

Self-defense is often our initial response to something we don't like about ourselves, which is one of the reasons developing self-awareness can be difficult.

For a brief while, let us go back in time to the year 1100.

We're writing down the qualities we think make a friend, partner, coworker, or family member unquestionably nice while seated at our wooden bench with our goose quill.

What items should we include on this nostalgic list? Most likely terms such as "patient," "kind,"

"faithful," and "generous," to mention a few.

Let's go back to the present now. We're typing the exact list while seated (or standing) at our desk. The virtues we would have written down in 1100 would likely still be there, but we might add some comparatively fresh ideas.

"Self-awareness" is a characteristic that I would want to have in a person—and to possess—and I would want to add it to my list.

But what does being self-aware actually mean? How did the legendary quality of self-awareness come to be, and how may one develop it?

The core of "self-awareness" is understanding and controlling our emotions.

It's possibly possible to link the word "self-awareness" to Freud and Jung, but in terms of contemporary usage, I believe it made a comeback about the time Daniel Goleman released "Emotional Intelligence," which was over twenty years ago,"

Rebuilding trust

writes author and clinical psychologist John Duffy.

According to Duffy, "the acknowledgment of one's emotional condition at any given instant in time is, in essence, self-awareness." According to the thesis, we frequently have a completely unconscious awareness of our current emotional state and how much it affects our behavior and cognitive processes. We are better equipped to control these other aspects of our lives to the extent that we can control our emotional states.

Marital and family therapist Amy McManus continues, saying that "self-awareness is [also] the ability to see to look at your own words and deeds from an external viewpoint; to perceive yourself as others perceive you.

This is how self-awareness functions as a method of introspection that allows one to evaluate external factors against their own emotions and actions rather than excluding them. It involves "meta-cognition: the ability to think about thinking [and] implies the ability to

perceive ourselves as we see ourselves, but also to grasp how others may see us based on what we know about human behavior," as licensed clinical social worker Katie Krimer puts it.

We frequently mistakenly believe that we are self-aware.

I am unable to count how I've written off a lot of people, including ex-boyfriends, by labeling them as "not self-aware." I say this as though I'm positively brimming with metacognition.

I could be mistaken about my level of self-awareness; a lot of us are.

"People frequently substantially overestimate their level of self-awareness, as social scientists have found," says Tara Well, an associate professor of psychology at Barnard College.

Many "believe that they know and understand themselves much better than they do," says Kramer. They might have even shied away from developing self-awareness because it calls for the most honest examination of

Rebuilding trust

oneself, which frequently results in difficult-to-handle feelings of shame.

Being self-aware is essential to living a happy life.

Either way, self-awareness is a crucial practice to grow.

"In the past, [a lack of self-awareness] might have been brushed off as a benign human quirk, but self-awareness is becoming increasingly important as our environment grows more complex," states Well. "Perhaps the most important ability we have to deal with our upcoming challenges is self-awareness."

"You are more than likely able to exert an effect on the emotional vibe of a family, a job setting, or a social interaction if you can manage your own emotions," continues Duffy. To sum up, having self-awareness can be quite helpful in leading a more conscious and contented existence.

Here are some pointers for developing self-awareness.

Here are some tips from mental health professionals on developing or improving self-awareness:

1. Take an interest in your identity.

"A person needs to be curious about oneself to be self-aware," says Parenting Pod psychologist and life coach Ana Jovanovic. "We still require route maps for the places that our bodies and thoughts inhabit. Everybody has certain roads they would rather not travel and those they think are worthwhile. What you're willing to investigate and experience will determine how far you can go on your self-discovery path.

2. Take down your barriers

Self-defense is often our initial response to something we don't like about ourselves, which is one of the reasons developing self-awareness can be difficult.

Rebuilding trust

Make an effort to let go of your need to defend yourself and your judgment. "Letting go of defensiveness and being open to viewing oneself differently from how you have always perceived yourself are the keys to becoming self-aware," according to McManus. This frequently entails having to be open to viewing oneself in a less-than-ideal manner.

3. Take a real look in the mirror

"I teach individuals how to use mirrors as a meditation tool that boosts their self-awareness," Well adds of his studies. When people first examine themselves, they frequently have harsh judgments. I show them how to change their viewpoint and use introspection to become more self-aware. They get new insights into how their thoughts are influencing them in real-time and learn to measure their attention and emotions; this simulates face-to-face interaction These need attentive listening and giving someone your whole attention.

4. Write in a journal about what makes you feel good.

"Starting this process of being mindful is a terrific approach to journaling," says licensed mental health clinician Celeste Viciere. "Reflect on your day while you write in your journal. What feelings do you have? If you experienced any bad emotions during the day, consider the possible factors that led to their emergence. If you are experiencing any good emotions, consider what might have made you feel that way.

5. Replace some of your screen time with social time.

"The average amount of time we spend alone staring at our devices now exceeds the amount of time we spend interacting with others in person," claims Well. According to science, we must reflect to cultivate our sense of identity in connection to others. We lose this crucial human mirroring when we spend more time alone ourselves and on our electronics. In our society, the signs of a lack of mirroring are becoming increasingly noticeable: elevated anxiety, diminished empathy, and extreme self-objectification (as exemplified by the selfie obsession). A call for increased self-awareness and introspection exists, if not an urgent cry.

6. Find out what people think about you

Not only should we practice our in-person social interactions, but we should also take some of this time to find out how our loved ones see us.

Krimer advises, "Talk to your closest loved ones and be brave enough to ask how they see you in different scenarios." Obtaining insight into how We can become aware of something that was previously invisible to us by the way we act or appear in specific circumstances. Also very helpful for this is therapy.

7. Furious with someone? Adopt a "third-person" viewpoint.

In the end, having self-awareness will help you manage your emotions and improve your relationships with others.

Professor of marketing and consumer psychology at St. Mary's College of California, Michal Strahilevitz, emphasizes the significance of recognizing when something or someone is upsetting you.

"You can feel justified because you're upset if you catch yourself getting angry," adds Strahilevitz. The experience will be very different for the person with you, though (second person). It will get better to try to put yourself in that person's shoes self-awareness, lessen defensiveness, and perhaps even enhance your rapport with that individual. People who tend to be self-destructive or who are very critical of themselves will find that the third person is especially helpful. If a sympathetic friend were observing your actions, what advice would you give? That would entail adopting a third-person viewpoint.

Rebuilding trust

8. Continue to assess yourself (as well as a list of feelings).

The best way, in my experience, to cultivate self-awareness is to take a moment to stop and ask yourself, "How am I feeling right now? " "What do I believe could be causing that emotion?" asks Duffy. "Although it may appear ridiculously easy, my clients find it to be very challenging in reality. Many must always have a list of potential feelings with them The simple responses, such as "I feel fine," "I feel horrible," and "I feel angry," are not very insightful or fruitful when they start this exercise.

IMPROVE IT Psychologists' advice on how to be "excellent" at gossiping

9. Never stop learning—the path never ends

Although this post should provide some advice, there is an abundance of amazing content available that can support you on your never-ending path to self-awareness.

Kramer suggests, "Read and learn about the psychology and techniques of self-awareness." "Be enthusiastic about learning new things since they will teach you things about yourself. There are a ton of amazing psychology books and workbooks available that support developing our self-awareness. School of Life is an amazing publishing house that specializes in books and uniqueness card sets that assist in elucidating the significance of developing self-knowledge and the effects it has on all other aspects of our lives in a straightforward, understandable, and astute manner."

How to Develop Self-Awareness and Why It's Vital

The majority of people believe they are fairly self-aware. But in the wild, self-awareness is an extremely uncommon quality. The majority of us frequently exhibit a lack of self-awareness, which can make us unproductive and unprepared to interact with others.

Rebuilding trust

It will be simpler for you to choose your battles and manage your professional and personal relationships the more self-aware you are. We'll go into more detail about self-awareness and its importance in this post. Next, we'll discuss some pointers to assist you in developing that.

An Overview of the Value of Self-Awareness

To put it briefly, self-awareness is the capacity to accurately assess your feelings, personality, and abilities. Surprisingly, a lot of people lack this fundamental ability, despite how simple it seems.

Let's imagine you have an assignment that needs to be finished by next Friday and you work in an office. But rather than starting right immediately, you put off starting the task until the very last minute, rushing through the completion of it. As a result, the project didn't quite work out as planned.

If you have self-awareness, you would probably admit when you messed up and try not to do it again. Going one step further, you may examine the reasons behind your procrastination, and then attempt to remedy them. However, if you are not self-aware, you could avoid taking accountability for your deeds or even fail to recognize the qualities that led you to that situation.

Setting aside instances, the following are some advantages of having a high level of self awareness for both job and personal life:

• It helps you to precisely evaluate your character qualities and skill set.

• Since you are aware of your weaknesses, you can improve in your line of work.

• It can help you manage connections more effectively in both your personal and professional life.

Being honest is key to being self-aware, at the risk of sounding

Rebuilding trust

like a self-help book. You're not being honest with yourself if you're constantly coming up with justifications for your shortcomings, which may indicate a lack of self-awareness.

If you want to become a better person, you must develop your self-awareness. You can use all of your self-control to address your shortcomings once you are aware of them. This should therefore make your life better overall.

Four Tips for Developing Self-Awareness

As we mentioned, honesty is a prerequisite for developing self-awareness. But it's a little more complicated than that. Let's discuss a few techniques for developing self-awareness.

It's important to note that you may probably feel more at ease with some of these recommendations than others, and that's okay before we go right in. The first objective is to implement at least one of them and continue with it for a long.

You won't start to see the advantages right away.

1. Engage in "mindfulness"

Overall, self-awareness and mindfulness are closely related concepts. When we discuss the contemporary interpretation of mindfulness, we mean the concept of being aware of your environment, thoughts, and emotions.

Put differently, a lot of people attempt to block out their feelings and thoughts during the day. Because of the pressures of modern life, you can find yourself disregarding some aspects of who you are in the hopes that they will go away on their own.

Nevertheless, this strategy rarely succeeds. Being attentive requires facing and addressing those unfavorable emotions and thoughts. This is how it can benefit you:

• Since you won't have to expend as much energy trying to ignore things, mindfulness can help you focus better.

Rebuilding trust

You'll be able to assess people and events according to their merits, which might help you avoid making snap decisions.

• Studies suggest that engaging in mindfulness practices helps lower stress levels.

You may practice being more mindful in a lot of ways. We're going to take a risk here, though, and suggest that you attempt mindful meditation. Although it may not be to everyone's taste, meditation has many advantages. It's not as difficult as you would think to dabble in the field of meditation. Furthermore, you are under no obligation to embrace the mystique unless you so choose.

2. Ask for Feedback From Your Friends and Work Colleagues In many cases, you'll have negative personality aspects that only become apparent once they're pointed out to you. The reverse is also true – you might be knocking the ball out of the park metaphorically, yet haven't stopped to notice how great you're doing. If you're serious about becoming more self-aware, one of the best things you can do is look to the people surrounding you and ask them for their honest opinions about your character and skills. Often, you'll get responses you weren't expecting, which can force you to take a closer look at yourself.

However, asking for feedback can be tricky, as many people won't want to offend you. This means you need to be careful about how you navigate the approach. Here's what we recommend: • Don't just ask people what they think about you. Instead, opt for more pointed questions that don't leave room for open-ended responses. • Try to avoid asking your coworkers for personal feedback, unless you happen to be close to them. • Don't try to force friends to answer your questions if they feel uncomfortable giving you feedback.

Many individuals will indeed feel awkward when you ask for their honest opinions. You must recognize this and refrain from pressuring the matter in certain situations. Even if all of your friends have to say about you,

Rebuilding trust

that's usually plenty to learn important things about how they perceive you.

Lastly, you must be receptive to criticism if you want this process to be successful. You will likely encounter some viewpoints that you disagree with, but if they aren't based on subjective truth, there's no need for conflict.

3. Record Your Thoughts and Emotions in a Journal

Many believe that journals are only appropriate for younger people. But they're more than simply a place to write down your crush on someone or what that jerk did to you when you were on break. Journals, on the other hand, can be useful instruments for recording your mental condition.

To better concentrate on our daily responsibilities, we frequently tend to ignore the past. This is frequently advantageous because thinking back on the past negatively affects our emotions and productivity. But keeping a journal of your emotions, even regularly, can help you gain a more accurate understanding of yourself.

We invite you to pull out your old journal and have a look at it if you kept one in the past. For the majority of us, experiencing Keeping an old notebook helps us reflect since it brings back memories of our previous ways of thinking. Of course, nothing is stopping you from establishing a diary right now if you don't already have one (you can even use WordPress for it). The following are some of the items we advise you to attempt and record:

• Any noteworthy occurrences in your life and your emotions surrounding them.

• Your response to a challenging circumstance (and whether you could have done better!).

• Any disagreements you've had with others and how you resolved them.

You have the freedom to keep your journal as simple or as complex as you like. Just try to

Rebuilding trust

persevere and set aside sometime each week to go over the previous few days. You should feel much better about yourself after going through this "recap" process and be able to think of methods to make both your personal and professional lives better.

4. Monitor Your Objectives and Your Advancement Toward Them

We discussed in the last part the benefits of journaling for understanding your personality and how you respond to situations. But we also believe it's critical to monitor your objectives and your progress toward achieving them. Monitoring data to assist in making well-informed decisions is becoming to greatly heighten your awareness of yourself.

It's a great ability to develop to set and stick to goals. Maintaining track of your objectives might also assist you in determining whether your priorities change over time. Since the person you were even a year ago is presumably significantly different from the person you are today, this is essential to developing self-awareness.

It's acceptable to make some adjustments if you ever feel that your long-term objectives no longer accurately represent who you are or what you desire.

After all, learning to adjust to change is a necessary skill for developing self-awareness.

You can track your goals more effectively by using the tried-and-true SMART approach. They're all about establishing a measurable endpoint that makes it simpler to track your development. In these circumstances, it's generally a good idea to reevaluate your priorities because motivation is frequently a major contributing factor to lack of success.

In summary

Highly self-aware leaders are frequently the finest. Knowing your advantages and disadvantages will help you can

Rebuilding trust

assist you in building stronger professional connections. You can even strengthen your areas of weakness with enough discipline, which will help you develop into a more complete person.

Self-awareness is beneficial not only in the professional world but also in leading a fulfilling personal life. For this reason, you ought to use these four suggestions to develop your self-awareness:

1. Practice awareness.

2. Request input regularly.

3. Record your ideas and feelings in a notebook.

4. Monitor your objectives and advancement toward them.

CHARTER 3:

Break Panicking in a relationship

What is panicking?

A quick, intense fear that overpowers reason and logical thought and replaces it with overpowering sensations of anxiety, uncertainty, and frenzied agitation typical of a fight-or-flight response is known as panic. Individuals may experience panic on their own, or it may appear unexpectedly in huge groups as mass panic (which is strongly related to herd behavior).

How is a panic attack put an end to it?

• Techniques

• Diminishing nervousness

• Assisting another individual

Requesting assistance

• Recap

Panic episodes can come on suddenly and be very strong. Relieving the symptoms of a panic attack can involve actions like deep breathing, grounding exercises, light exercise, or repeating a mantra.

Although panic attacks are not always predictable, having a strategy for what to do in their event might help make someone

Rebuilding trust

feel more in control and help them cope with panic episodes.

This article discusses how to prevent panic attacks, general techniques for lowering anxiety, and how to support someone who is experiencing a panic attack.

13 methods to avert a panic attack

Both mental and physical symptoms can result from panic episodes, such as:

- perspiring

- Breathing quickly

- A pounding heart

- Anxiety and fear-related feelings

- persistent, severe worry

- a feeling of impending disaster

Here are 13 techniques that people can employ to help them regain control and lessen panic attack symptoms.

1. Remind yourself that it will pass.

Though it may seem unsettling at the moment, it can be helpful to realize that these emotions are temporary and won't hurt you physically during a panic attack.

Try accepting that this is a transient state of focused anxiety that will pass quickly.

Within ten minutes of starting, panic attacks usually reach their climax, after which the symptoms start to get better.

2. Inhale deeply

Breathing deeply can be advantageous. panic attacks and anxiety disorders sufferers, according to Trusted Source.

Breathing becomes shallow during panic attacks due to chest constriction and fast breathing. Breathing shallowly might exacerbate tense and anxious feelings.

Rebuilding trust

Rather, make an effort to breathe deeply and slowly, paying attention to each breath. Inhale deeply from the abdomen, filling your lungs gradually and steadily as you count to four on each breath.

One more option is to attempt 4-7-8 breathing.This includes:

• inhaling for four seconds.

• exhaling deeply for seven seconds.

• Take eight slow, deep breaths.

3. Take in a lavender scent

A Brief 2019 According to a reliable source, those with preoperative dental anxiety experienced a drop in blood pressure when they inhaled lavender oil.

A 2019 assessment of the literature indicates that using lavender oil orally and through inhalation may help reduce anxiety.

Individuals can dab or hold the oil on their noses and gently inhale their surroundings can aid in grounding them.

One stimulus can become less prominent when one is the focus. The object's shape, maker, and feel may all come to mind while the user examines it. This method can assist in lessening panic attack symptoms.

One useful tool for helping those who experience recurrent panic episodes stay grounded is a specialized, well-known object. This could be a hair clip, a tiny toy, a smooth stone, or a seashell.

These kinds of grounding practices might be helpful for those who are coping with anxiety, trauma, and panic attacks. Additional grounding methods can be:

• imagining a secure location

• Putting music on or concentrating on other sounds in the vicinity

• emphasizing the senses

6. The Five-4-3-2-1 protocol

Rebuilding trust

A person experiencing a panic attack may feel cut off from reality. This is because anxiety can overwhelm other senses in its intensity.

The 5-4-3-2-1 approach is a mindfulness practice and a grounding technique. It assists in shifting the person's attention from stressful situations.

People can apply this method by carefully and slowly completing each of the following steps:

• Examine five distinct objects: Take a moment to consider each of these.

• Pay attention to four different sounds: Think about where they originated from and what makes them unique.

• Touch three objects and think about their uses, textures, and temperatures.

• Separate the scents: This could be the aroma of soap, coffee, or laundry detergent on clothing.

• Identify one taste you can experience: Try eating a piece of candy or pay attention to the taste in your mouth.

7. Say the slogan aloud

A mantra is a word, phrase, or sound that can offer strength and focus. One way to lessen anxiety, tension, and panic is to mentally repeat a mantra.

The phrase might be as straightforward as "This too shall pass," and it might serve as comfort. It might represent something more spiritual to other people.

A person's bodily reactions may slow down while they concentrate on softly repeating a mantra, enabling them to control their breathing and release tension in their muscles. Walk or engage in a little exercise.

A person can escape a stressful situation by walking, and the rhythm of the movement may also assist in breathing control.

Engaging in physical activity releases endorphins, which are substances that calm the body

Rebuilding trust

and elevate mood. Regular exercise can help Trusted Source gradually lower anxiety, which may lessen the frequency or intensity of panic attacks.

9. Experiment with muscular relaxing methods

Tension in the muscles is another sign of a panic attack. Using muscle relaxation exercises could help prevent an attack. Rapid breathing and other symptoms may lessen if the mind perceives that the body is relaxing.

Progressive muscle relaxation is a well-liked and successful approach. A reliable resource for managing anxiety and panic episodes.

This entails tensing and relaxing certain muscles one after the other. One can accomplish this by:

1. Maintaining the tenseness for five seconds.

2. Saying "calm down" while letting go of the muscle.

3. Before going on to the next muscle, give the affected muscle ten seconds to relax.

10. Visualize a joyful location.

A place where one feels calm, secure, and at ease should be a happy spot. Each person will have a different specific location.

Shutting your eyes and visualizing yourself in this location can be helpful when an attack starts. Consider how serene that place is. Additionally, people can picture themselves stepping barefoot on soft rugs, scorching sand, or cool earth.

11. Take all prescription drugs as directed.

Depending on how bad the panic attacks are, a medical professional might advise Trusted Source to take a "use-as-needed" drug. These drugs usually take effect quickly.

A beta-blocker or benzodiazepine may be present in some. A beta-blocker called

Rebuilding trust

propranolol (Inderal) lowers blood pressure and pauses a rapid heartbeat.

Doctors frequently recommend alprazolam (Xanax) and diazepam (Valium) as benzodiazepines for panic attacks.

Nonetheless, patients should take these drugs precisely as directed by their doctor because they have the potential to become quite habit-forming. When used with alcohol or narcotics, they can have potentially fatal side effects.

Selective serotonin reuptake inhibitors (SSRIs) are another medication that a doctor may recommend. These can help stop panic episodes before they start.

12. Inform someone

If you find that certain places, such as your employment or social circle, are the trigger for your panic attacks, it could be beneficial to let someone know and let them know what type of support you can provide if it happens again.

Informing someone else about an attack that occurs in public can be helpful. They might be able to find a peaceful area and keep others from swarming in.

13. Recognize your triggers

Some things can set off panic episodes regularly. It may be possible for people to lessen the frequency and severity of panic attacks by learning how to control or avoid their triggers.

Possible causes could be:

• confined areas

• throngs

• Financial problems

• Speaking in front of an audience

• Rebuttals

On the other hand, some people could suddenly get panic attacks without any particular reason.

• shut your eyes and pay attention to your breathing.

Rebuilding trust

In a few minutes, you should start to feel better. Afterward, you can feel worn out.

 an additional breathing technique to serene fear.

Strategies to avoid having panic attacks

Professor Salkovskis advises, "You need to try and figure out what specific stress you might be facing that could make your symptoms worse." "It's crucial that you don't limit your daily activities and motions."

Act

• Use breathing techniques daily to help stave off panic episodes and ease them when they do occur.

• Engage in regular exercise, particularly cardiovascular exercise, to help you reduce stress, relax, elevate your mood, and increase your self-confidence.

• Consume meals frequently to stabilize your levels of blood sugar

• Steer clear of coffee, alcohol, and tobacco as they might exacerbate panic episodes.

• Attend a panic support group to obtain practical guidance on how to control your panic episodes. Your doctor can connect you with local groups.

To recognize and alter the unfavorable thought patterns that are causing your panic episodes, consider undergoing cognitive behavioral therapy (CBT).

Give, Take Care of, and Mend Relationships: Guidelines for a Caring Exchange

It takes work to build a loving connection. They change with time. Whether your relationship developed more gradually from a strong friendship or as an unexpected, love-at-first-sight eruption, If you want anything to last, you must devote all of your attention to it.

Rebuilding trust

If you remember these three important reminders, you can continue to be in a loving relationship: share, care, and mend relationships.

Caring and sharing are evident. But fix? Why would you need to mend a good relationship? Relationship repair is essential from the start to maintain the things you love about your connection, just like sharing and caring.

Distribute

You share your life just by existing together. Beyond that, openness and honesty are essential in loving partnerships. The quality of your connection is based on how much and how frequently you share.

In addition to having sex and being physically close, loving couples exchange intimate and sentimental feelings. You also feel more secure and like you belong in the relationship when you are willing to open up to the other person about your innermost passions, worries, hopes, and disappointments.

Physical Closeness

Understanding your partner's sexual preferences and expressing your own are essential components of sharing physical intimacy. Make it known that reciprocal enjoyment is what matters most to you. Experiment and try new things. Keeping your sex life fresh is important. Relationship pleasure is frequently well-predicted by a strong sexual connection.

Closeness on an emotional level

In a loving relationship, partners communicate not just via spoken words but also through perceiving and skillfully handling the feelings that underlie those words. Verify with your partner regularly. Find out how your spouse is feeling.

Does your significant other appear anxious? Recognize your partner's cues. What symptoms point to bewilderment, anger,

Rebuilding trust

frustration, or sadness? Which exhibit happiness and pleasure?

Observe your partner's tone of voice. Recognize nonverbal cues. Attend to the silence that surrounds you. You can better comprehend your partner's perspective by being attuned to their emotions. This awareness allows you to react in a kind and considerate manner. Talk about your problems as well. Above all, express your gratitude for your partner's actions and identity.

Talking About Your Secrets and Fears

Establish a secure space for you to confide in your partner about your issues. Honesty demands outcomes and trust.

in a greater degree of trust. You become closer and your relationship gets stronger when you are vulnerable with each other.

Develop trust consciously. Try to be as giving as you can. Make a compromise offer. Don't forget to establish and uphold boundaries. Don't coerce your spouse into doing tasks they don't want to. Combat disagreements amicably. Recognize how your partner's wants and objectives align with your own.

You can honor each other and strengthen your loving relationship by telling each other your secrets.

Take Care

The Advantages of Being a Carer

A loving relationship is based on tenderness and caring. Furthermore, both the caregiver and the person receiving care gain much from this. Looking after someone releases oxytocin, sometimes known as the "love hormone," a brain molecule. It has to do with sex, relationships, empathy, and trust. Positive emotions and energy arise from giving and receiving love touches and hugs.

Providing Mutual Support

Rebuilding trust

Encourage one another and express your support with words and deeds. Kind words and compliments go a long way toward boosting your partner's confidence. Tell your lover how wonderful they are. And repeat the action frequently. Never assume anything about one another.

Little Deeds Add Up

Demonstrate your concern in both modest and significant ways. Small actions have a big impact. How does your significant other feel loved? When do you experience love? Back rubs, strolls with your partner, unexpected gifts; listening to a love song, letting them sleep late, preparing their favorite dinner; reading a poem; playing a favorite game; and gazing up at the stars together.

In essence, when you and your spouse repeatedly engage in these modest, considerate actions, you express your gratitude and encourage you both to focus on the good aspects of your relationship.

Fix

Observe Trends and Identify Triggers

Relationship issues frequently come up again. Communication and behavior patterns develop, such as one spouse being protective and the other being critical of the other. When one partner acts disrespectfully, the other partner withdraws.

Finding these tendencies is the first step in mending a relationship. Identify the things that set off disputes. Be aware of body language cues.

and vocal intonation. Observe your feelings. Let's pause, regroup, and get back to normal before carrying on with the conversation.

Regain Control and Strengthen Your Promises

You are grownups now. You are able to identify and manage your feelings while assisting your partner in taking back control of

Rebuilding trust

theirs. Accept accountability for your feelings and acknowledge your part in the issue. Then use constructive means of expression to communicate.

Additionally, try not to assign blame for failures. blaming your partner's characteristics for a problem ("You forgot again. That's quite characteristic of you") weakens ties to the cause. Be it via forgiveness, appreciation, confidence-building, identifying strengths, or expressing thanks, you will strengthen your bond.

Drama

You both share a past with your significant other. Your relationship is a multi-chapter story. Remain focused on the issue at hand rather than bringing up historical examples.

Adults don't need to act as martyrs or victims. It's not necessary to maintain a score. Communicate your thoughts and feelings to your partner without placing blame. Try to focus on the solutions you can implement to solve the issue.

Remind yourself of the positive things in life.

People that are happy look for the good. Examine your partnership to see what functions well. Selecting to focus on the positive rather than the negative initiates a chain reaction of kindness.

One of Mark Twain's proverbs is, "Wise choices originate from encounter. Poor decision-making leads to experience. Treat the process of mending your relationship with kindness, sincerity, and an open mind. Try again if your conduct blows up.

Share, care, and repair are three equally important pieces of relationship pieces of advice.

Your relationship will grow if you share your secrets and experience both physical and emotional intimacy. Small acts of kindness and reciprocal support will fortify it. Observing trends,

Rebuilding trust

identifying triggers, practicing self-control, reaffirming commitment, being in the moment, avoiding drama, and emphasizing the positive are all part of relationship rehabilitation. This kind of maintenance will keep your partnership strong and developing.

If you find it difficult to implement these ideas, don't be hesitant to ask for assistance. A helpful first step in building the kind of relationship you want is couples therapy.

CHARTER 4:

Deepen intimacy in a relationship

Intimacy and love are the foundations of any successful partnership. It's the tiny things, like sharing a kiss, holding hands, a playful bum slap, or laughing over a shared inside joke, that you share with your significant other.

Because of how hard life may be at times, it might be simple to lose the close bond you two have during life's ups and downs. Thus, how can you bring it back to life and make it deeper than before? You can thank me later! Please continue reading to understand the five essential stages!

Step 1: Recognize the Four Cs of a Good Relationship

The Four C's of a Healthy Relationship are consideration, compatibility, communication, and consideration. These are the essential characteristics that I found to be crucial to any successful and long-lasting relationship during my research.

• Consideration: This is crucial since maintaining a healthy and long-lasting relationship requires a high level of emotional intelligence and self-awareness. You also need to be conscious of the need to take into account your partner's wants and feelings. The more committed you both are to building a wonderful relationship, the more driven you both are to show consideration for one another.

Rebuilding trust

• Compatibility: I view compatibility as the relationship's navigation system; the more compatible you two are in terms of values, goals, beliefs, sex, priorities, intelligence, emotional intelligence, and other areas, the easier it will be for you to navigate life together. There will be variances in every relationship, which makes it the ideal setting for learning about one another and yourself. In my opinion, this is a perfect example of where the 80:20 rule works. 20% of differences, 80% alignment.

• Communication: Once more, a lot of people underestimate the importance of effective communication in relationships. It's about how you express your needs, wants, and—most importantly—how you handle conflict. Different partners and relationships will always handle conflict resolution differently; the more similar your styles are, the easier you'll resolve situations.

• Collaboration: This is the way you work as a couple, the truth is most couples are co-dependent and that creates so much insecurity and a lack of true connection. The difference between a co-dependent and a healthy interdependent relationship is individual accountability of emotions, happiness, goals, and life in general. In co-dependent relationships often one or both partners make their partner accountable for these things which creates a toxically enmeshed relationship.

Step Two - Create Space In Your Relationship To Connect & Have Fun

Life can get so unbelievably busy, from waking up in the morning and checking your phone straight away in bed, to busy days at work, to crashing out together in the evenings. Are you getting the finest qualities from one another?

It's time to establish small routines that will help your relationship grow. Whether it's sharing dinner and discussing your day's events over a ten-

Rebuilding trust

minute spoon before getting out of bed in the morning or spending an entire weekend day together trying something new to create memories of new experiences, there are many different ways to foster these kinds of relationships.

Setting aside time for scheduled date nights might also be a great idea since it shows that you both value each other. Since actions usually speak louder than words, it's crucial to understand that you mean something to your spouse and that they mean the same to you.

Step 3: Recover Emotionally Or From Past Traumas tense situations

You won't believe how much pain and emotionally charged situations can sever a relationship and keep people from truly connecting. We've all heard of the "anxious" and "avoidant" attachment styles; yet, most of the time, these are signs of trauma that require immediate attention and healing.

Anxious attachment styles are characterized by behaviors such as chasing, neediness, insecurity, and emotional instability. These behaviors are not random; rather, they stem from the trauma of not having their emotional needs satisfied as children. This can be a difficult idea for most people to understand. It is possible to have a happy childhood without having your emotional needs satisfied.

Similarly, avoidant attachment styles might result from a sense of worthlessness of being loved, being afraid of love, fearing that you aren't good enough for the person they are with or they can pick partners that they feel they won't fully fall in love with.

The other type of trauma that most people don't talk about is hypervigilance - this can harm relationships because hypervigilance can cause people to be either really reactive or very shut down. Most people who are in a relationship with a partner who has hypervigilance will feel like they are unable to say anything or they will be

Rebuilding trust

attacked or shut down, or feel like they are treading on eggshells which doesn't create the right environment for love, and intimacy to grow.

Step Four - Discover Your Styles Of Connecting

So many people assume that we all communicate the same way and that we all have the same needs. That's not the case at all.

You may have heard about Love Languages and that's a great way People tend to assume that everyone has the same needs and communicates in the same manner. That is just untrue.

Perhaps you've heard of love languages, and that's a fantastic approach.

Hypervigilance is another kind of trauma that most people don't discuss, but it can seriously damage relationships since it makes people overly reactive or reclusive. The majority of individuals who are in a relationship with someone who is hypervigilant will feel as though they can't express

themselves, that they will be attacked or shut down, or that they are walking on eggshells, which doesn't foster the kind of atmosphere that is necessary for closeness and love to blossom.

Step Four: Find Your Own Unique Connecting Styles

People tend to assume that everyone has the same needs and communicates in the same manner. That is just untrue.

I'm sure you've heard of love languages and that's a terrific place to start learning about the connection between you and your spouse, but there are more subtle aspects to this as well.

Say words of affirmation are your partner's preferred method of communication. The problem is that not every compliment will elicit the same response, so are you aware of the precise words to use to make your lover feel unbelievably wonderful? We discuss just that in The Levels of Love Mastermind.

Rebuilding trust

Step Five: One of the Main Obstacles to Intimacy and Love

Pardoning. Yes, you were the first to hear it. Before their partner does something unexpected, a lot of people have the preconceived notion that their relationship is flawless and that they are incapable of doing anything wrong.

Among the elements that establish security and the capacity for both partners to forgive one another as well as themselves is a prerequisite for safety in a partnership. Enjoying unconditional love as a flawed human being is safe when done correctly.

In actuality, it's critical to give yourself enough time to comprehend the events that transpired as well as the motivations behind the acts when something negative occurs in a relationship. For instance, you would undoubtedly react to the same circumstance quite differently if someone attempted to emotionally harm you than if they had no such goal. Understanding how to heal from both small and large setbacks is crucial since intention truly alters the way we view every circumstance.

A fascinating fact is Relationships and building healthy, connected relationships truly are an art and a science. Take some time to forgive one another and assess any unresolved hurt, resentment, or anger that may be simmering beneath the surface. I promise that when you let go of these things, your relationship will become closer and more loving immediately. Take your time incorporating these things into your relationship and watch how it develops and grows, and how your love and intimacy with your partner deepens. The truth is that everyone deserves to experience greater levels of love and intimacy, but not many people know how. For this reason, I'm hosting a FREE Masterclass on How To Discover & Grow More Intimate & Deeper Love Levels

Rebuilding trust

intimacy in a partnership

In a relationship, intimacy is the state of being near, emotionally supported, and linked. It entails having the ability to communicate a wide spectrum of human emotions, ideas, and experiences. It entails expressing your thoughts and feelings to someone else, letting down your guard (becoming vulnerable), and sharing your aspirations and feelings with them.

Establishing and sustaining intimacy takes time and patience on the side of both partners. Finding intimacy in a relationship with someone you love can be one of the most fulfilling experiences.

In addition to sharing intimate moments with someone, you may also be intimate in all aspects—intellectually, recreationally, monetarily, spiritually, creatively (like remodeling your home), and during difficult times (like cooperating as a team).

When we grow close to someone and receive confirmation that they love and accept us for who we are, that person becomes our intimate partner. Typically, children grow close to their parents and peers. In close interactions with other adults, friends, family, and a spouse, adults yearn for intimacy.

Sex and intimacy

No matter how wonderful their sexual experiences may be, it's crucial to communicate a wide spectrum of feelings with a partner; otherwise, some people start to feel alone and lonely.

Many couples associate intimacy and emotional closeness with the act of "making love." Intimate sexual relationships require vulnerability and mutual trust. Other types of intimacy, such as emotional and spiritual intimacy, are associated with closeness during sexual activity. Only a portion of sexual intimacy, which also includes foreplay and other physical closeness, is sexual.

Consider ways to express love and affection without having sex, but keep in mind that sex

Rebuilding trust

encompasses a variety of bodily interactions. A couple's relationship is typically more gratifying the more intimate they are with one another outside their sexual lives turned into Difficulties in creating intimacy

Some couples find it difficult to achieve intimacy in their relationship. Others can find that after achieving intimacy it seems to slip away. There are many reasons why some people find it difficult to achieve intimacy in their relationship. This is commonly the result of problems such as:

•   communication issues – if you and your partner are not communicating to each other what your feelings and needs are, then they are not likely to be met. If you do not feel understood by your partner then intimacy is hard to create or maintain. It's important to talk to your partner about what you need and to check in with them about how they are feeling. This act alone can create a feeling of being connected to an intimate intimacy and connection

• dispute: It might be challenging to grow close in a relationship where there is a constant dispute. Feeling connected to someone you are at odds with is not simple. Anger, hurt, anger, distrust, or a feeling of undervaluation can all have an impact on intimacy. Seek assistance if your relationship is suffering from strife.

Take a class or workshop that will assist you and your spouse in resolving some of your interpersonal issues.

• Keep in mind that developing and sustaining intimacy is a necessary component of a happy relationship and that it is natural to experience ups and downs in your partnership.

6 Strategies to Strengthen Your Close Bond with Your Spouse

Have you ever thought that there wasn't enough intimacy or connection while having a strong attraction (high chemistry) toward your partner? Perhaps you're wondering if there's anything more you can do to

Rebuilding trust

improve your relationship and why you're not feeling fulfilled in it. This could occur for a few different causes.

Let's compare maintaining a relationship to caring for a garden. To thrive, they require regular sunlight, watering, and a specific amount of fertilizer and de-weeding. The garden's potential appearance simply heightens your imagination.

Some plants require more care than others, thus when it comes to caring for the garden, assigning responsibilities should be based on each plant's advantages.

The best relationships are those in which both partners put in the time and effort to nurture the relationship and are willing to make adjustments as needed, much like caring for a garden. At that point, it turns into an experience that the two of them jointly design and carry out.

Attraction and affection are necessary for you to feel a deeper, more intimate connection with your companion. The length of a relationship is nearly entirely determined by having one over the other. The sexual and romantic yearning that drew you two together is the foundation of the attraction. The love and concern that binds you together is affection. If the flowers in your yard are the source of appeal, then caring for them and providing nutrients would be affection.

Following that, there are numerous methods to improve the closeness of your partnership. There are many other types of intimacy, including sexual, emotional, romantic, intellectual, and so forth. Establish each person's priorities and work from there. Whether you're dating someone new and still getting to know them better or you've been with a long-term partner(s) and want to reignite the spark, these ideas will undoubtedly strengthen your relationship.

1. Honest and Open Communication to Foster Belief

All the intimacy categories revolve around communication,

Rebuilding trust

and self-reflection is essential because it helps you identify your desires and craft better messages.

Investigate what you think you need to feel more connected to your spouse, and then figure out how to tell them what you need. Allow children to express their wants and needs as well.

For instance, while thinking back on sexual closeness, it's crucial to be able to tell your spouse what you're craving—more foreplay, cuddles, pillow chat, etc. It can be challenging to communicate at times, particularly in younger partnerships. If that's the case, you might want to think about using a card game as a fun method to start more personal chats. I discovered this card game called "Connect," which is meant to be played by couples to have conversations about various subjects that matter and which promote intimacy and connection. You can either utilize some of these prompts from the deck as thought starters or buy your deck online.

What I find most admirable about you is...

• What do you believe grateful friends might be celebrating about us when they talk about us?

• At the end of each day, how about getting back together again?

• The key to comprehending why I can occasionally be challenging is to keep in mind that

This game will allow those of you whose partner or partners are somewhat mysterious to tell you more about them. Try the other ways to engage with them first if they don't like the notion.

2. Use the Love Languages of each other.

The author of "The 5 Love Languages," Gary Chapman, identified five common ways that romantic partners communicate and feel love. It's common to believe that our significant other shares our need for affection, which can cause

Rebuilding trust

dissatisfaction and disappointment if your thoughtful actions are not as well remembered. Words of affirmation, deeds of service, receiving gifts, spending quality time, and physical touch are the five ways we experience love. In the long run, your partner won't be happy if you continually buy them pricey gifts when they prefer quality time together and you are too busy working to provide it to them.

3. Give Longer & More Kisses

To increase attraction and bonding, replicate those intense movie kisses. According to a 2013 study published in the Archives of Sexual Behavior, a couple's assessment of the quality of their relationship is positively correlated with how often they kiss, and more kissing is associated with greater reported levels of happiness. However, the longer a relationship lasts, the less often you kiss. According to research, one in five couples never even kiss. Thus, make kissing a regular part of your relationship, and try not to forget the most memorable kissing moments you shared early on.

Usually, kissing occurs initially before having further sexual relations activities. It allows you both more time to develop that sexual anticipation and helps you determine your sexual compatibility and desire for this person before sex. Though kissing to initiate sex may not always work out well when one person is not in the mood and would rather connect in other ways, be aware of the motivations behind your kisses. A symbol of affection is kissing during intercourse and throughout the day.

4. Examine sensuality without aiming for a climax

Speaking about sexual connection, take your time getting to know each other's bodies and imaginations without focusing just on getting an orgasm. By being patient with one another, you will come to value each other more on an emotional and a physical plane.

Rebuilding trust

Recalling my gardening analogy, flowers require time to develop before they open up. Savor each development that gets you one step closer to realizing the greatest potential of the partnership and your bond.

Effective communication is crucial when discussing the kind of foreplay that you enjoy and those that don't pique your interest as much. You might use the following suggestions for your upcoming improved foreplay session:

• Try massaging each other's entire bodies with oil.

• Utilize role-playing to introduce some fantasies

• Without intending to do more, experience physical closeness by cuddling and conversing in the location that you most often identify with sexual intimacy.

5. Consult a Sex or Couples Therapist for Advice

Perhaps there are more deeply ingrained issues that keep us blocked from deepening our connection and receiving counseling can reveal our own (or our partner's) fears of intimacy or more fully understand what is going on.

6. Form New Relationship Habits

To conclude, my final suggestion is to use all this advice to develop new habits in your relationship. If you don't like the way things have been flowing, then changing a few behaviors might just improve the whole pattern. For example, instead of jumping out of bed to take a shower immediately after sex, lay there for a while and enjoy the afterglow together. Talk about what you enjoyed the most from the experience to keep it lasting longer. Develop a shared morning or evening ritual that allows you to expand upon the type of intimacy or affection you need most and elaborate on the kind of closeness or love you most require.

The goal of this post was to highlight a few of the numerous strategies you can employ to strengthen your bond with your partner. If you feel stuck, seek outside advice from a therapist who specializes in relationships and sex. Be creative and test what works best for you and your partner(s).

CHARTER 5:

What Is Autonomy: (The Importance of Autonomy in Relationships)

The idea of autonomy in relationships isn't talked about or explored as much in marriages and romantic relationships as it ought to be.

Most people view romantic relationships and marriages through rose-colored glasses, seeing them as constant companionship, flexibility, tenderness, and compromise.

And if the above-described ideas are crucial for romantic long-term commitment, autonomy is just as crucial.

What does autonomy entail in love relationships and marriages, then? An autonomous relationship: what is it? Is it significant? Is there a distinction in the relationship between autonomy and independence?

These are merely a handful of the numerous significant queries about partnerships and autonomy that you may have.

Remain calm.

You will undoubtedly get insight into striking a healthy balance between connection and autonomy in your marriage or relationship as you make your way through the process of developing and preserving autonomy in romance and commitment.

What autonomy means in relationships and commitment

This intense desire to spend as much time as possible with one's beloved is often a defining feature of the early stages of any romantic engagement. I take it that this was also very much the case in your love relationship.

Rebuilding trust

And you know what, this is a perfectly natural and acceptable phenomenon!

But as a romantic relationship develops and grows, and that tremendous desire and attraction start to fade a little, the need for autonomy becomes increasingly important.

In a partnership, emotional autonomy is synonymous with autonomy. It seems beautiful to think of one soul living in two bodies, their lives so deeply entwined and dependent upon one another.

In a long-term committed relationship, autonomy allows both parties to have meaningful interactions outside of the romantic partnership, such as hobbies, purpose, academic and professional responsibilities, and valued interpersonal relationships with friends, acquaintances, and family.

In a relationship, autonomy does not mean that there is always a power struggle between the partners. No. It is about discovering meaning, fulfillment, and purpose in your life—even if it isn't a love relationship.

Take a look at this fascinating perspective on attachment and autonomy before continuing:

The value of independence in romantic and married relationships

After going through the definition of autonomy in relationships in detail, let's examine the exceptional significance of autonomy in committed love partnerships.

One of the main factors affecting the quality of your marriage or romantic relationship is relationship satisfaction. The best way to maximize relationship satisfaction is to be autonomous in your partnership.

Your demand for competence and autonomy is satisfied when you are in an independent relationship. For this reason, having autonomy in a relationship is essential to improving your devotion to your partner.

Rebuilding trust

Autonomy in relationships is essential for fewer disagreements and more effective conflict resolution between the couples, in addition to greater commitment to love.

You will both feel content and pleased in your relationship when you and your partner are independent in your connection with one another. Both partners' general well-being will improve.

It will also guarantee that, when you are not in your autonomy connection, you both feel competent and adequate.

What it means to be in a relationship without autonomy

After discussing the importance of autonomy in relationships, Now would be an excellent moment to talk about what a partnership looks like without individuality.

If you recognize any of the following indicators of a lack of autonomy in a relationship, you may comprehend the lack of autonomy in romantic relationships:

You and/or your partner experience an intense desire to put each other's needs first. This implies that you will both be prepared to give up everything of your wants, hobbies, passions, and general well-being to appease the other.

Your beloved's life and schedule center around yours, and vice versa.

You can start to mistrust or question the validity of your feelings for your partner and your love relationship.

Being oneself in a relationship feels uncomfortable and undesirable.

When there is a lack of autonomy in a committed relationship, one or both partners find it difficult or offensive to discuss setting appropriate limits. Boundaries fuzziness sets in.

Both physically and emotionally, your connection is tiring.

Five tried-and-true strategies to

Rebuilding trust

keep your romantic connection autonomous

At last, we can tackle the crucial query: "How can one maintain their independence in a romantic partnership?"

The following five practical methods may help you preserve autonomy in your marriage or love connection if you'd like to be more cognizant of it:

1. Self-awareness is essential.

Working on your self-awareness is one of the first things you can do if your relationship is already naturally autonomous and you wish to maintain this positive relationship habit.

Autonomy in love is based on having a clear sense of who you are. To prevent any loved one from tarnishing your sense of self, make sure you keep up your boundaries.

2. Preserve your social structure

Maintaining your autonomy in relationships also means continuing to make time for the people you care about. Both with and without your lover, you are welcome to see your loved ones.

Arrange to spend time with them and allow yourself to create priceless memories with your loved ones. This will enable you to find fulfillment in relationships that aren't romantic, and you know what?

By sharing these memories with your loved one, you can express your delight to them.

3. Cherish your alone time.

You should value your private space. Sometimes it can become extremely unhealthy to spend every minute of the day with your partner.

This is an excellent moment to learn more about your history and how you have changed over time. It is vitally crucial to understand who you are and retain your sense of self to enhance the lifespan and health of your relationship.

Rebuilding trust

4. Self-calming

You should always be able to depend on yourself first when things get tough. It might lower your self-esteem and make you appear incompetent if you rely too much on your partner for everything.

You must identify your own sources of support and Get independence in your manner. You will never truly be happy if you live your life according to someone else's terms.

5. Continue to pursue your interests and passions

Your hobbies and passions shape who you are as a person and what defines your true self.

It is not necessary to combine your interests with someone else's just because you are in a romantic relationship; you still have the freedom to do and say whatever makes you happy, no questions asked.

Make time for those pursuits and embark on these personal explorations by yourself. It will assist you in becoming more self-aware and in harmony with your body and mind.

Five tested strategies to achieve and build autonomy in your romantic connection

As previously said, maximizing relationship satisfaction in a marriage requires autonomy. Now, let's talk about how you can establish your own life while still gaining autonomy in your partnership and instilling a strong sense of contentment and happiness!

Here are 5 tried-and-true strategies for becoming independent:

1. Value your uniqueness as well as that of your partner.

To begin with, doing everything in your life as a pair is not a fantastic idea. Having different hobbies and interests between two people in a relationship is

Rebuilding trust

perfectly acceptable and even encouraged.

Divergent viewpoints don't always result in conflict! Nevertheless, Similar core values should underpin variations in viewpoints, views, etc. Enough room exists!

2. Time spent alone is essential.

This means that you should schedule times of free time when you and your partner each spend time doing your own thing regularly. There is no greater significance than giving your mate space.

And consider it this way: after your alone time, you can return to each other feeling renewed and revitalized. This may be as easy as reserving a couple of hours at a spa! Go alone and unwind.

Additionally, whenever you return to you You two will be able to appreciate that time together with mindfulness, my love.

3. Motivate one another to engage in activities

Just do it if you've always wanted to take up a hobby like baking or playing an instrument! Encourage your spouse to pursue a passion if he has ever mentioned doing so!

You will both be able to give each other space if you encourage each other to pursue these interests apart!

4. Spend time with loved ones (separately).

An additional useful strategy for fostering some autonomy in relationships is by making contact with your family members. Urge your spouse to make contact with their family.

Schedule time apart to spend with those you love. To be independent, one must have a solid social network and support system.

5. Guidance

Rebuilding trust

Choosing to get counseling is a great method to create independence in your love life. Take your significant other to see a psychologist or counselor, and choose couple's counseling.

In addition to couple's counseling, individual psychotherapy is a valuable option for fostering self-awareness and personal development.

In summary

Put these previously discussed tactics into practice and give your romantic life liberty. Make the proper balance and get ready!

Why relationship autonomy matters and how to foster it

Being social beings, humans desire acceptance and assistance. To feel like you're delivering your most genuine self to every connection, you must also put your personal needs and objectives first.

It can be difficult to strike the correct balance between dependence and independence, and it frequently begins with how you feel about yourself. However, cultivating autonomy in your relationships may be the secret to having happy, fulfilling bonds.

What does autonomy mean in a partnership?

According to a 2019 study, being autonomous in a relationship means acting in a way that satisfies your desires, feeling genuine, and making your own decisions and principles.

The self-determination hypothesis states that having an independent and self-aware feeling is a learned behavior that you develop as a young adult, even when one spouse or friend may support your autonomy more than another.

Growing up helps you develop a distinct sense of who you are. At this point, you start experimenting with being independent, establishing

Rebuilding trust

personal boundaries, and figuring out how your environment makes you feel most at ease.

You can feel like you can handle anything life throws at you by strengthening your sense of self and directing your actions toward your goals. However, you may feel unhappy and out of sorts if you feel compelled to act in ways that are inconsistent with your principles.

When you believe that your Your relationship decisions are in line with your requirements, and you feel fulfilled on the inside, which spills over into other aspects of your life.

According to the 2019 study, persons who feel in control of their relationships are more motivated to engage in healthy habits that uphold their relationships and have a higher feeling of overall well-being. According to additional studies, those who experience autonomy also:

• Recover from disagreement more quickly and employ more effective coping mechanisms

• Engage in happier social exchanges

• Show less defensiveness and self-destruction

How does an independent connection appear?

The foundation of an independent relationship is transparency, respect, and support for one another. It calls for introspection and emotional

intelligence to accept authenticity, recognize and respect other's boundaries, and establish positive communication relationships.

Being autonomous is not the same as being distant or alone. Instead, it's the capacity to exercise self-governance and make decisions that honor your needs and desires. A partner who values your autonomy will affirm and encourage your development on both a personal and interpersonal level.

Rebuilding trust

Remarkably, the same 2019 study discovered that a good partnership requires more than just autonomy. Your sense of togetherness, or relatedness, makes up the other half.

The two are inextricably related. You're more inclined to form close bonds with those who appreciate your autonomy. Additionally, you're more inclined to respect your partner's decisions if you have a stronger connection to their independence.

In every aspect of your life, you can have autonomous partnerships. Here are some possible images of those. In a professional setting

Interactions with supervisors and coworkers may inspire you to apply for jobs or give your all at work. Good relationships at work can motivate you to work together, exchange ideas, and provide a hand, which can boost your job satisfaction and garner support from your coworkers.

Here are some examples of how workplace autonomy could look like:

• Your manager pushes you to live up to your basic principles, such as striking the correct work-life balance.

• Your partner gives you the confidence to take chances, trust your gut, and grow from your errors

• Your team respects your time rather than relying on you to handle every issue at work.

• Your direct report speaks with empathy and a productive manner, acknowledging your point of view.

In a romantic partnership

Research indicates that partners who can realize their potential and accomplish both individual and shared objectives report greater levels of relationship satisfaction and overall well-being.

A spouse who supports your independence could:

Rebuilding trust

- Honor your boundaries, alone time, and personal space.

- Discuss your life decisions, future aspirations, and relationship values.

- Honor your interests, successes, and personal development.

- Motivate you to cultivate deep social ties and support systems

- Choose actions that will satisfy your needs, wants, and emotions surrounded by loved ones and friends

Since the majority of your relationships are probably with your friends and family, it's critical to establish a sense of independence with this group.

Your family members may support your independence by:

- Increasing your sense of self-worth and ease in your skin

- Confirming your relationships, career, and lifestyle choices

- Respecting your personal space and boundaries

- Encouraging your independence away from the partnership

How does one demonstrate a lack of autonomy?

Here are some instances of what a lack of independence could look like in your interpersonal relationships to help you better grasp the significance of autonomy:

1. You put other people's needs, feelings, or time before your own.

2. Your buddies violate your boundaries, personal space, or privacy

3. Your boss pressures you to put in excessive hours.

4. A family member criticizes you for who you are.

5. When making decisions, your partner doesn't take your thoughts, desires, or opinions into account.

6. Your supervisor closely monitors your job

Rebuilding trust

7. You frequently experience stifling and discontent in your romantic relationships.

8. You require other people's approval before making decisions for yourself.

9. You rely on other people to provide your emotional needs, sense of self, or self-worth.

10. You purposefully withhold information out of fear of mockery

How can self-governance promote personal development?

Building wholesome relationships that value individual individuality necessitates having tough talks, introspection, and compromise.

Let's imagine your business partner frequently makes significant choices without seeking your input, perhaps steering your company in a way you find unsettling. You get the impression that your opinions are unimportant, invalidated, and dismissed. However, the thought of facing them makes you feel nervous and irritated.

Resolving will necessitate significant personal development. You need to examine yourself, examine your feelings, and comprehend how your emotions influence your ideas and actions to stand up for yourself and establish healthy limits. That isn't always simple. You could remain silent, but that would probably make you feel angry, unsatisfied, and possibly aggressive.

Now, picture yourself sitting down to discuss business with your partner. They may feel that you micromanage their responsibilities, have a different idea of what constitutes an important decision, or fail to recognize your feelings of exclusion. To stay in contact and maintain alignment, you jointly determine which decisions require collaboration and create new lines of communication.

You can promote personal development through that action and introspection. As a result, you can voice your opinions, see things from your

Rebuilding trust

partner's point of view, and perhaps feel more comfortable handling conflicts in the future.

Eight strategies for fostering autonomy in a pair

Respecting one another's autonomy is a continuous effort that calls for a dedication to each person's unique life. Should you like to start fostering greater self-sufficiency in your relationships, consider these eight suggestions:

1. Promote open communication: Develop the habit of accepting honest, forthright communication to discuss needs, concerns, or desires in a setting that is secure and judgment-free. You'll feel more at ease discussing and being open the more compassionately and empathically you treat each other.

2. Honor differences: Take pleasure in what makes the other person special. People will feel free to be who they are and ask for what they want if we accept their diverse viewpoints and personalities.

3. Foster extracurricular activities and social networks: Acknowledge that you are unable to meet everyone's needs and interests. To make them feel content and supported, encourage them to pursue their other passions and connections.

4. Be respectful: Respect for one another is based on acceptance of one another's limits, beliefs, and identity. Respect them by observing any boundaries they impose and accepting them for who they are.

5. Promote self-care: Acknowledge the other person's need for introspection and personal development. Acknowledge that practicing

Rebuilding trust

self-care is not always simple; encourage them when they succeed and support them when they fail.

6. Show vulnerability: By being honest with your spouse about your feelings and fears, you may inspire them to show you their true selves. It might also promote empathy, deeper ties, and trust.

7. Steer clear of codependent behavior: Pay attention to any tendencies toward codependency that cause you to feel anxious or as though you are unable to be who you are. Watch out for excessive dependency on your emotional support as well as a lack of independence and boundaries.

8. Identify your goals: Without a clear understanding of your needs and desires, it is impossible to advocate for them. Establish your objectives, perhaps through journaling or meditation, and check in frequently to make sure your close relationships aren't impeding your Encourage independence to build connections

Knowing the value of autonomy in a relationship enables you to recognize the characteristics of wholesome relationships. Additionally, gaining this liberty allows for priceless personal development, such as learning to advocate for yourself and supporting your colleagues to exchange ideas.

Every relationship is different and needs its exchange of reciprocity. It takes time to find the ideal ratio of independence to connectedness in your love relationships, professional ties, and friendships.

However, you'll feel closer if you learn to accept one another's independence. Additionally, you will appreciate each other's autonomy even more as you get closer.

Rebuilding trust

CHARTER 6:

Maintain trust and safety in a relationship

Why and How to Develop Trust in Your Relationship

It is impossible to overestimate the value of security, comfort, and loyalty.

Strong trust is one of the most consoling things you can have in a relationship, but it takes time and intentionality to build.

In a relationship, trust is a result of feeling secure and devoted to your spouse. It's the cornerstone of a strong relationship, according to clinical psychologist and Yeshiva University professor Sabrina Romanoff, PsyD.

"To trust someone is to depend on them because you feel secure in their company and know they won't mistreat or abuse you. Because it enables you to be open and vulnerable, trust is the cornerstone of partnerships, without needing to defend yourself defensively," adds Romanoff.

Quick Overview

Relationships depend heavily on trust, and when it's lacking, negativity, conflict, insecurity, sadness, and worry can result. To be vulnerable and let your guard down with one another, it's critical to work with your spouse to develop trust in your relationship.

You can get assistance from a therapist or couples counselor if you are struggling to work through your trust issues with your partner.

The Significance of Trust

Relationships that are fulfilling and fruitful require trust.1. This is how it can improve the quality of your relationship.

Encourages Happiness

Relationships require trust because it makes it possible to be more frank and generous. You are more likely to be

Rebuilding trust

understanding of your partner's flaws or annoying behaviors if you trust them Overall, you have faith in them and are aware of their support for you.

Lessons Tension

You can also handle disagreement when you have trust. When you trust your partner, you feel allied in areas that are most important to you, so you are more inclined to overlook issues or make a commitment to finding solutions.

If you trust your spouse, you are more likely to find the good in them and be willing to give them the benefit of the doubt even if they do something disappointing.

Boosts intimacy

Building trust forges a solid connection and a solid base from which to grow. A sense of trust with your partner fosters a closer, safer relationship. You feel secure knowing that your partner has your back when you have mutual trust in return and are dependable in providing consolation, attention, and assistance.

Encourages Joy

As it enables you to be more forthcoming and open in a relationship, trust is crucial. Because you have faith in them and know they will always have your back, you are more ready to forgive your partner for their inadequacies or annoying habits.

lessens conflict

You can handle confrontation when you have trust. Because you feel united in certain areas, when you trust your partner, you are more inclined to put up with problems or dedicate yourself to seeking answers that are most important to you.

If you trust your spouse, you are more likely to find the good in them and be willing to give them the benefit of the doubt even if they do something disappointing.

Rebuilding trust

Effects of a Lack of Trust

Building trust takes time, so if your partner persistently fails to if they don't fulfill pledges or obligations, you'll start to have low expectations from them.

You'll start to realize that your partner is unreliable when their statements and behaviors diverge. Recurring transgressions or persistently harmful actions undermine confidence.

Many issues might arise in a relationship due to a lack of trust.2 Lack of trust might also have the following negative effects on your mental health:

• Lack of intimacy: Intimacy in a relationship tends to decline when trust is low. You should probably keep your distance from your dishonest partner— both physically and emotionally.

• Negativity: You can become obsessed with the idea that your spouse has harmed you, which will make you distance yourself from them and feel resentful of them. This may hinder intimacy and bonding.

• Insecurity: Relationship insecurity is typically the result of a lack of trust. As a result, you will continuously question what your spouse says, and you might respond by taking charge more, which could drive them even farther away. For example, persistently contacting or messaging your partner to monitor them may cause them to become distant.

• Depression and anxiety: When there's minimal trust in a relationship, you may feel more depressed or anxious all the time since you'll be wondering if your partner is telling the truth or not being dishonest.

• Difficulty focusing: When you don't trust someone, it can be difficult to focus, particularly if you're always assuming the worst or wondering what they're thinking, feeling, or doing.

Rebuilding trust

• Distress: Betrayal, trauma, and emotional dysregulation are among the mental, emotional, and physical symptoms of not being able to trust your partner.

• Fear: Anxiety and fear can be a result of low trust. It's possible that you're scared of what your spouse will do next or that you won't be able to count on them in difficult times.

• Loneliness: Feelings of loneliness and isolation are inevitable when you don't trust the person who is closest to you.

How Can a Person Gain More Trust in a Partnership?

You can take a variety of actions to encourage trust in your relationship. Romanoff offers some practical strategies.

Enhance Errors

Being open and truthful when one another hurts you or violates expectations is a crucial first step in developing trust.

Everyone is prone to error. Ultimately, what matters is that once you've fixed whatever went wrong, you two will be able to grow closer and learn from each other. To do this, it is best to take full responsibility for them and demonstrate how you will improve going forward.

Have Open Communication

Since secrecy erodes trust, you can feel more at ease and start to lower your guard when your spouse can be open and honest while providing space to discuss subjects that may cause you to lose faith in them.

You will feel more connected to your lover the more you can align yourself. You can talk about relationship problems more easily when there is open communication between you. You will feel more connected to your lover when you can communicate freely.

Rebuilding trust

Ways to Establish Trust Again

If there has been a breach of trust in your relationship, there are steps you may take to repair the intimacy, connection, and trust. Actions you can do:

• Have an open mind and a desire to improve the connection.

• Together, create new, fulfilling experiences.

• Have conversations with one another

• Look for methods to communicate

• Express your true feelings and mean what you say.

• Honor and fulfill the promises you make.

• Maintain consistency

• Ask questions to learn more about your spouse and your relationship with them, and listen to them empathically.

• Keep developing your self-awareness so that you can communicate your needs, wants, and thoughts in the most sincere way possible.

•Acknowledge and take responsibility for mistakes made, apologize for the harm done, and be clear and specific about how things will be approached differently in the future

Patience is also important. It may take time to rebuild trust, but continuing to work toward improving your relationship can help you eventually mend those damaged connections.

• HEALTH

• FITNESS

• BEAUTY

• LIFE

• RELATIONSHIPS

How To Build Trust In Your Relationship And Why It's Important, Per Relationship Experts

What's hard to build, easy to ruin, and essential to any healthy intimate relationship? Trust. Your connection may start with a meet-cute and a spark, but for a

Rebuilding trust

relationship to have real staying power, you've got to be able to use the "T" word when describing how you feel about your partner.

Theresa Herring, a certified marriage and family therapist, states that "you'll need to prioritize creating and sustaining trust if you want a healthy, happy, long-term relationship." "Intimacy and connection on an emotional level cannot occur without it."

Building trust is not something that just happens, like many other crucial things in life. It requires a lot more practice than just a couple of jumping exercises from high school. However, the outcome is far superior. First of all, you'll feel protected, hugged, and genuinely loved. You'll also know that your individual won't let you down should things go wrong.

The unfortunate truth is that trust is a sensitive topic. Everybody enters relationships having had past experiences, even if those experiences involved possible breaches of trust previously. (Excesses, thanks for nothing.)

But, you should be aware that you can still have, well, trust in your relationship despite whatever may have happened in the past. "It's always better to take the risk and trust someone until they prove they're not trustworthy," says PsychAlive senior editor and clinical psychologist Lisa Firestone, PhD.

Are you prepared to dive right in? Continue reading to learn everything you need to know from dependable relationship professionals about developing trust in your partnership.

What does trust mean?

People perceive the word "trust" differently, and it's one of those concepts that you frequently can't put into words until you experience it. You are aware of when you You can tell when you don't trust your partner.

According to professional marital and family therapist Shawntres Parks, "Trust is the feeling of emotional, bodily, and

Rebuilding trust

psychological security established when a person is consistent with their behavior."

According to Firestone, the degree to which you feel your spouse will help you in times of need determines how much you can trust them. You want to be able to know that you can always rely on your significant other (S.O.) in times of need, no matter how large or small, more than just feeling confident in their words. "We put our well-being in the hands of another person in our love relationships, which is a fairly dangerous idea," she says. And it is undoubtedly beneficial to have the assurance that your special someone will support you in times of fear.

Why is developing trust important?

You will feel happier and more secure as a couple overall if you take the time to build that link because trust is the cornerstone of many successful relationships. When there is trust, "everything else feels a little easier and safer," according to Herring.

Having said that, the following are some particular justifications for why it's critical to develop trust in relationships:

1. It lessens hostilities.

In a relationship, everyone wants to feel at ease and ease—and not only when they're snuggling on the couch and binge-watching their favorite program. However, do you know what doesn't promote harmony? feeling that you have to keep an eye on everything that your significant other is doing, or fearfully speculating about their whereabouts when you're apart. The likelihood that those heightened emotions may surface at an inappropriate time increases with their accumulation. (And at that point, typically communicated ineffectively.)

Relationship therapist and sex researcher Dr. Sarah Hunter Murray, PhD, RMFT, states that "having trust in our relationships simply means that we have security in our relationships." "That usually implies we feel less

Rebuilding trust

tense, on edge, and hypervigilant, and more at ease and peaceful."

2. Trust allows individuals to follow their path.

You and your partner don't have to always want to spend the same weekend activities or follow the same after-work schedule just because you're dating. When you trust each other, you may go about your own lives with the assurance that you will reconnect and enjoy each other's company later on.

According to Murray, "trusting our spouse means that we give them the freedom to be themselves." Murray says, "That means we give them the freedom to think what they think, feel what they feel, and make decisions about what they do, without continually observing, interrogating, or passing judgment on them."

3. A closer connection results from trust.

You have to put yourself out there when you reveal your actual self to someone, be it your strange eating habits or your worst anxieties. In a relationship, having a foundation of trust does make being vulnerable easier, albeit it's not an easy ask of you or your spouse little simpler because, in Murray's words, "we get to be our real selves, our partner gets to be their authentic selves, and as a result, we get to connect authentically."

How can one develop trust in a romantic partnership?

Not sure where to begin? WH asked a few professionals for advice on fostering trust in relationships. And just to remind you, you should encourage your spouse to read this as well since it contains advice just for you two.

1. Always be there for them.

It is beneficial to have someone to bear the brunt of life's blows alongside you. It's crucial to

Rebuilding trust

prioritize your partner's emotional needs and be there for them throughout these times.

"It's easier for your spouse to trust you with their emotions if they know you'll acknowledge their feelings and not get defensive," adds Herring. You likely desire a companion who will support you during difficult times.

2. Show interest and responsiveness.

You know when you've said all you have to say about how you're feeling and then you realize no one is paying attention? It's pretty much the worst sensation ever, isn't it? It's also definitely not a good strategy to develop trust.

Parks advises, "Be alert and sensitive to your partner's feelings and experience when you are conversing or spending time with them." "Using both your verbal and nonverbal cues to demonstrate that you are paying attention to your spouse and that you value the opinions they have to say." This implies that, yes, you have to put down your phone occasionally. (You'll make it!)

3. Show dedication and constancy.

It takes brick after brick after brick to make a sturdy house that has a homey feel to it. Similar to this, relationships require regular, devoted action that, in the long run, can save you a great deal of worry and uncertainty.

"Repeated efforts are necessary to establish a positive connection in a relationship," according to Parks. Commit to following through on your commitments—not simply for the sake of getting a pat on the back. Long-term benefits come from consistency.

4. Connect with your most exposed self.

Brust slam those walls, darling! It can be uncomfortable, painful, and even frightening to share

Rebuilding trust

personal details, but you have to take a chance for the biscuit. It's a terrific method to feel more at ease with your lover, even if it might not come naturally to you at first.

"I believe it's such a misconception that people think of vulnerability as weakness," Firestone adds. A person cannot truly be attuned to you if you are closed off to them. How can they learn anything about you? Alternatively, you don't truly feel loved and accepted if you're suppressing aspects of who you are. You feel loved and accepted for the image of yourself that you present, not for the real you." Observed.

5. Make quality time a priority.

Yes, indeed, Yes, this is yet another instance where it's best to put down your phone. But if all you do together is watch TikToks together, it's unlikely that you'll build a strong sense of trust. It entails setting aside time specifically for one another so that candid and sensitive discussions can take place.

According to Parks, "making quality time a priority gives you more opportunities to practice being emotionally available, responsive, and involved." "You and your partner can develop knowledge about your own boundaries and relationship expectations by spending quality time together."

"If all you do together is share TikToks, you won't build a strong sense of trust."

6. Establish limits.

You get to set appropriate limits and determine when your business is exclusively yours, even when you love your spouse unconditionally and when participation is possible. Establishing limits will enable your partner to treat you in the manner that you desire. Your partner will likely say or do something that crosses one or more of your limits if you don't know them, according to Parks.

Don't wait to bring it up until your significant other crosses a barrier. Determine your

Rebuilding trust

boundaries on your own for a while, and then schedule some time in your calendar to talk about them with your spouse.

"You could express to your lover that you value their time. I would appreciate you informing me if you anticipate being late so that I can modify my schedule appropriately."Parks recommends. Certainly easier said than done, however because of this Talking takes place before any boundaries are crossed; it's completely non-aggressive.

7. Show one another respect.

Although it may seem obvious, there's a reason this is on the list. Yes, that's the first rule of humanity, but far too often, we take it for granted. According to Herring, "Belittling, condemning, and yelling erode trust—fast." "Over time, it may become nearly difficult to rebuild."

Establish ground rules for your debates because that's when things tend to get disrespectful. Decide to never turn to the

behaviors you find intolerable. Therefore, if it involves calling each other names or swearing at each other in a heated argument, decide which behaviors you want to avoid and follow your ground rules.

Do you want to learn even more about your partner Try posing one of these queries to them.

8. Honor your obligations.

Of course, things happen in life, and occasionally you have to postpone your date due to an unforeseen issue at work. However, make every effort to attend the events you have committed to, particularly those that you have scheduled well in advance. You are honoring your commitment to them if you follow through on the agreements you make with them.

Herring advises, "Say what you mean and do what you say." "It helps a lot if your partner knows they can rely on you."

9. Own up to your mistakes.

Rebuilding trust

I apologize; it is inevitable. Murray emphasizes the significance of owning up to your mistakes and extending an apology when you are at fault. To stop additional uncertainties Murray gradually suggests that, to provide that extra confidence, couples should check in more frequently than they may need to and be more accountable to one another.

10. Stay receptive to criticism.

This does not imply that you and your spouse should compile a long list of all the things that irritate one other. But when it comes to the big things, Firestone believes it's critical that a couple feel comfortable being honest with one another and having productive conversations about their problems.

11. Discuss problems as they arise.

Don't hold your tongue when something in the relationship annoys you. Even while you may believe you're being helpful to your partner, you'll probably wind up venting your frustrations later on in other, worse ways. Nobody desires to be the one who broods over a casual remark made three months prior and then suddenly launches an unjust dispute.

In this manner, "your partner can more readily be there for you, and they won't have to worry that a terrible mood is about them," according to Herring. "Timely and effective communication is key to building trust."

What happens if I don't trust people?

You're not the first (or last) in a relationship if you bring a few trust concerns with you. Furthermore, there are instances when your problems are unrelated to your present relationship.

According to Firestone, "I think trust issues are tricky because they largely revolve around whether a person is acting in a

Rebuilding trust

way to build trust." However, there's also the matter of what you bring to the relationship and the degree of trust you possess given your formative experiences."

"Being honest with your partner is the only thing you can do."

There's nothing you can do but tell your lover the whole truth about what's going through your mind. Herring advises being upfront with your partner about how you feel and what you need from them to prevent defensiveness. She claims, "They'll reinforce the uneasiness you're already feeling if you make it about their behavior." "Make it more personal by putting your emotional needs first." Do you get it?

After trust is lost in a relationship, how can it be regained?

If you remove one piece of the relationship jigsaw, the other pieces of trust might fall apart faster than in a Jenga game. "We can lose trust in our partner if they start acting more secretively or differently out of nowhere without satisfactory explanations, or if they don't keep their word, fall in a pattern of forgetting to call or show up on time, or if they seem to give conflicting details or mixed messages," says Murray, although cheating is the most obvious example of how someone can lose trust in their relationship.

CONCLUSION

Although it's so ethereal, discovering true love is one of life's most wonderful experiences. Before concentrating on romantic relationships explicitly, we will first provide a quick explanation of what love means in various kind of relationships in this article. Since falling in love and loving someone are two separate experiences, we'll also discuss the differences between the two. Continue reading for our in-depth explanation of what love in relationships means.

There are various forms of love, and each one is legitimate. When most people think of love,

Rebuilding trust

they think of romantic connections, yet true love may also be felt for friends, family, and even pets. Forming diverse emotional connections is an essential aspect of the human experience.

Generally speaking, love is having a great concern for someone since you You don't have to feel that way; you can choose to. You simply act.

In the end, falling in love is an extremely private process. Not everyone experiences or looks the same, and that's okay.